It!

PLANES and CHOPPERS

LYN A. SIROTA

WORLD BOOK

This World Book edition of *Planes and Choppers*
is published by agreement between
Black Rabbit Books and World Book, Inc.
© 2018 Black Rabbit Books,
2140 Howard Dr. West,
North Mankato, MN 56003 U.S.A.
World Book, Inc.,
180 North LaSalle St., Suite 900,
Chicago, IL 60601 U.S.A.

Marysa Storm, editor; Grant Gould, interior designer; Michael Sellner,
cover designer; Omay Ayres, photo researcher

Cataloging-in-Publication Data is available at the Library of
Congress.

ISBN: 978-0-7166-9351-2

Printed in the United States at CG Book Printers,
North Mankato, Minnesota, 56003. 3/17

BOLT

Image Credits

Alamy: age fotostock, 24–25, 26;
CPC Collection, 4–5; Hideo Kurihara,
22–23; Images-USA, 19; Mark Hamilton,
Cover; MixPix, 8; Stocktrek Images, Inc., 17; VDWI
Aviation, 18; commons.wikimedia.org: Altair78, 28
(Boeing); Ken Hackman / US Air Force, 28 (Blackbird);
KGG1951, 11; TSRL, 28 (Galaxy); iStock: inhauscreative,
32; jondpatton, 7; Shutterstock: 19srb81, 17 (camo), 26
(camo); BigMouse, 7 (turbine), 10, 18 (turbine), 24; Emili-
aUngur, 1; EQRoy, 12; Marina Zezelina, 14–15; MyImages
- Micha, 28 (Chinook), 31; My Portfolio, 29; tai11, 3,
20–21
Every effort has been made to contact copyright
holders for material reproduced in this book.
Any omissions will be rectified in subse-
quent printings if notice is given to
the publisher.

CONTENTS

CHAPTER 1

RULERS
of the Sky

A plane speeds through the sky. Shortly after being seen, it is heard. The plane is flying faster than the speed of sound!

Planes and helicopters rule the sky. They come in many shapes and sizes. Some are for military use. Others carry **civilians**. Read on to see how some of the best compare.

CHAPTER 2

The AIRCRAFT

SR-71 Blackbird

The Blackbird came out more than 50 years ago. But it still holds records today. It is the world's fastest plane. It's the highest flying too. The Blackbird is a **stealth** plane. **Radar** cannot pick it up. The U.S. Air Force used it to gather information. Soldiers flew it over other countries. They took pictures of the territory. The Air Force retired the plane in 1999.

range
how far an aircraft can fly on one tank of fuel

RANK IT!

about
2,200 miles TOP SPEED
(3,541 kilometers) per hour

weight
59,000 pounds (26,762 kilograms)

RANGE
about **3,682 miles**
(5,926 km)

HEIGHT **18.5 feet**
(6 meters)

AIR MOBILITY COMMAND

C-5M Super Galaxy

The Galaxy is the United States' largest military airlifter. Its job is carrying aircraft and cargo. It can carry up to five helicopters. It has a total of 28 wheels. They help spread the plane's weight out evenly. The plane loads from the nose and rear. Soldiers drive vehicles in and out.

RANK IT!

TOP SPEED
about
591 MILES
(951 km) per hour

weight
400,000 pounds
(181,437 kg)

HEIGHT
65 feet
(20 m)

range
about
8,055 miles
(12,963 km)

Newscopter R44

The Newscopter is popular with TV stations. Its equipment allows it to act as a reporting studio. Its cameras show action in detail and color. The chopper can record, send, and receive footage.

RANK IT!

TOP SPEED
about 130 miles (209 km) per hour

weight
1,673 pounds (759 kg)

RANGE
about 345 miles (555 km)

HEIGHT 10.75 feet (3 m)

Boeing 747-8

The 747-8 is huge! It is one of the largest nonmilitary planes. It is 250 feet (76 m) long. Boeing made the first 747 in the 1960s. People called it the first jumbo jet. Many different 747s have been made since then. The 747-8 is one of the newest. It can carry 410 passengers.

RANK IT!

TOP SPEED
more than
660 MILES
(1,062 km) per hour

weight
485,300 pounds
(220,128 kg)

HEIGHT
63.5 feet
(19 m)

range
about
9,206 miles
(14,816 km)

cockpit

fuselage . . .
(body)

wing

rudder

flaps

Mikoyan MiG-29

The MiG is a fighter plane. The **Soviet Union** developed it. The plane can make sharp turns. It launches attacks at low and high speeds. Its targets can be in the sky or on the ground. The plane's radar isn't the best, though. Poor radar means the pilot must be especially skilled.

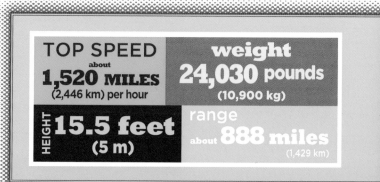

TOP SPEED
about
1,520 MILES
(2,446 km) per hour

weight
24,030 pounds
(10,900 kg)

HEIGHT
15.5 feet
(5 m)

range
about **888 miles**
(1,429 km)

UH-60 Black Hawk

More than 20 countries use Black Hawks. It's easy to see why. Black Hawks are dependable and strong. Militaries use them to carry troops. They're also used in rescue missions. Their cargo hooks can lift vehicles. Armored seats protect the pilots.

RANK IT!

TOP SPEED
about 174 miles (280 km) per hour

weight
11,516 pounds (5,224 kg)

RANGE
about 368 miles (592 km)

HEIGHT 17 feet (5 m)

Bell 206L4

Bell choppers have many uses. Firefighters, police officers, and business people all use them. Emergency medical workers rely on Bell choppers too. They use them to get people to hospitals quickly. The chopper has a powerful engine. It has a large area for seating too.

RANK IT!

TOP SPEED
about
144 MILES
(232 km) per hour

weight
2,331 pounds
(1,057 kg)

HEIGHT
10 feet
(3 m)

range
about **374 miles**
(602 km) fully loaded

PARTS OF A HELICOPTER

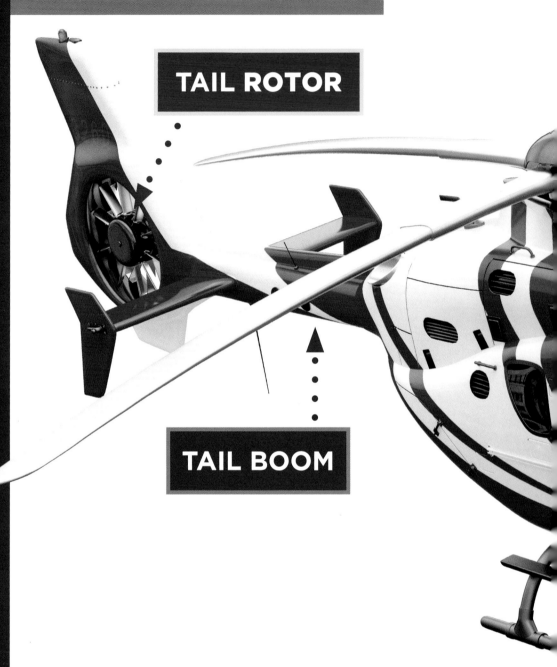

TAIL ROTOR

TAIL BOOM

COCKPIT

ROTOR BLADE

LANDING SKIDS

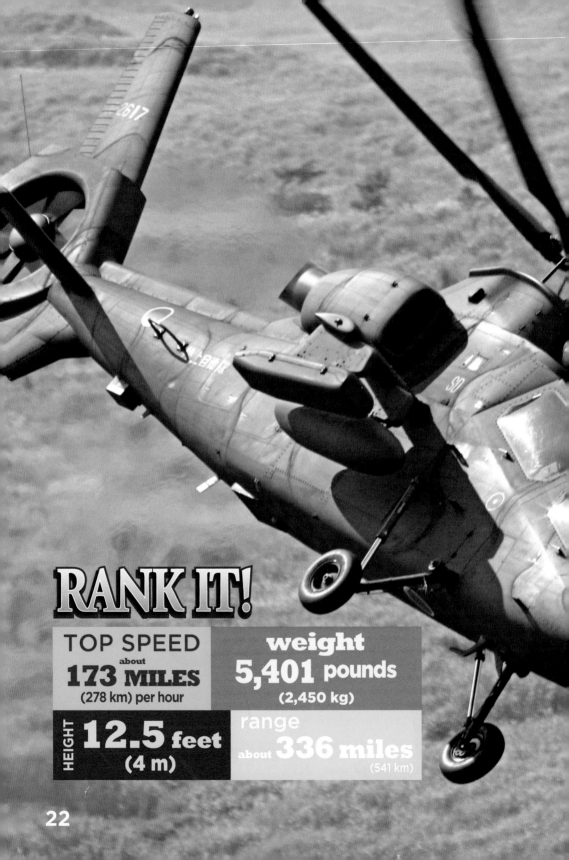

RANK IT!

TOP SPEED
about **173 MILES**
(278 km) per hour

weight
5,401 pounds
(2,450 kg)

HEIGHT 12.5 feet
(4 m)

range
about **336 miles**
(541 km)

Kawasaki OH-1

This military chopper is from Japan. Soldiers mainly use it for **scouting**. It's small and light. It is sneaky too. The OH-1 isn't nearly as loud as other choppers. A special tail rotor keeps the chopper quiet. This chopper is nicknamed "Ninja."

F-22 Raptor

The Raptor is perfect for **combat**. It is fast and ferocious. The Raptor has high-tech sensors. They allow the pilot to find threats. The pilot can fire onboard weapons at attacking enemies. The plane has stealth and speed on its side. It is used for air and ground missions.

RANK IT!

TOP SPEED
about 1,535 miles (2,470 km) per hour

weight
43,340 pounds (19,659 kg)

RANGE
about 1,850 miles (2,977 km)

HEIGHT 16.5 feet (5 m)

Comparing Wingspans

FEET

- 250
- 200
- 150
- 100
- 50

Boeing 747-8	C-5M Super Galaxy	SR-71 Blackbird	F-22 Raptor	Mikoyan MiG-29
224 feet (68 m)	223 feet (68 m)	55.5 feet (17 m)	44.5 feet (14 m)	37 feet (11 m)

PLANES AND CHOPPERS

CH-47 Chinook

The Chinook (shi-NOOK) came out in the 1960s. Soldiers first flew it in the **Vietnam War**. And soldiers still use it today. In fact, the militaries of 19 countries use the Chinook. It's one of the fastest military choppers. It's strong too. Its center hook can lift 26,000 pounds (11,793 kg)!

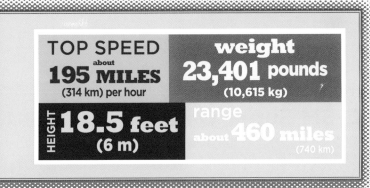

TOP SPEED
about
195 MILES
(314 km) per hour

weight
23,401 pounds
(10,615 kg)

HEIGHT
18.5 feet
(6 m)

range
about **460 miles**
(740 km)

CHAPTER 3

Weight

485,300
(220,128 kg)

400,000
(181,437 kg)

59,000
(26,762 kg)

43,340
(19,659 kg)

24,030
(10,900 kg)

450,000
400,000
350,000
300,000
250,000
200,000
150,000
100,000
50,000

| Boeing 747-8 | C-5M Super Galaxy | SR-71 Blackbird | F-22 Raptor | Mikoyan MiG-29 |

Height

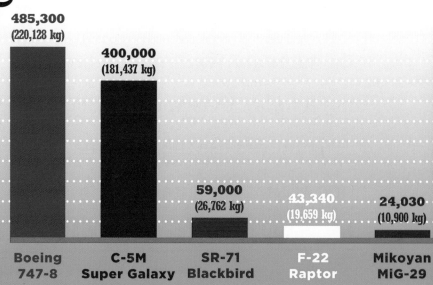

CH-47 Chinook
18.5 feet (6 m)

SR-71 Blackbird
18.5 feet (6 m)

Boeing 747-8
63.5 feet (19 m)

C-5M Super Galaxy
65 feet (20 m)

RANK IT!

Check out how they stack up!

23,401 (10,615 kg)	**11,516** (5,224 kg)	**5,401** (2,450 kg)	**2,331** (1,057 kg)	**1,673** (759 kg)
CH-47 Chinook	**UH-60 Black Hawk**	**Kawasaki OH-1**	**Bell 206L4**	**Newscopter R44**

RANGE

about **9,206 miles** (14,816 km)	about **8,055 miles** (12,963 km)	about **3,682 miles** (5,926 km)
Boeing 747-8	**C-5M Super Galaxy**	**SR-71 Blackbird**

Top Speed

SR-71 Blackbird	**F-22 Raptor**	**Mikoyan MiG-29**
about	about	about
2,200 miles (3,541 km) per hour	**1,535 miles** (2,470 km) per hour	**1,520 miles** (2,446 km) per hour

GLOSSARY

civilian (si-VIL-yuhn)—a person who is not a member of the military or of a police or firefighting force

combat (kahm-BAT)—active fighting, often in a war

radar (RAY-dar)—a device that sends out radio waves for finding the location and speed of a moving object

rotor (RO-tuhr)—spinning blades that support a helicopter in the air

scout (SKOWT)—to get information about someone or something

Soviet Union (SOH-ve-uht YOON-yun)—a former country in eastern Europe and northern Asia

stealth (STELTH)—an aircraft design that is hard for radar to pick up

Vietnam War (vee-et-NAHM WAWR)— a conflict between 1954 and 1975 between South Vietnam and the Vietcong and North Vietnam

BOOKS

Garstecki, Julia. *Military Aircraft.* Military Tech. Mankato, MN: Black Rabbit Books, 2018.

Peterson, Judy Monroe. *All about Planes.* Let's Find Out! Transportation. New York: Britannica Educational Publishing in association with Rosen Educational Services, 2017.

Willis, John. *Helicopters.* Mighty Military Machines. New York: AV2 by Weigl, 2017.

WEBSITES

All about Airplanes and Flight
easyscienceforkids.com/all-about-airplanes-and-flight/

Fun Flight Facts for Kids
www.sciencekids.co.nz/sciencefacts/flight.html

Military Aircraft
www.dkfindout.com/us/transportation/history-aircraft/military-aircraft/

INDEX